NEGOTIATION

MASTERY

*Strategies, Techniques, and Ethics for
Successful Negotiations*

Alex Grean (Dr)

TABLE OF CONTENT

assertive approaches for handling competitive counterparts, you will gain a comprehensive toolkit to tackle any negotiation challenge with confidence and finesse.

We will also address the unique challenges and difficult personalities that you may encounter during negotiations. Armed with practical strategies, you will be equipped to navigate high-stakes situations, manage emotional dynamics, and handle contentious counterparts with grace and effectiveness.

Additionally, we will explore advanced negotiation techniques that will take your skills to new heights. Techniques such as persuasion, influence, and negotiation in complex scenarios will further elevate your negotiation prowess, enabling you to secure optimal outcomes in even the most challenging situations.

Finally, we will delve into the ethical dimension of negotiation and emphasize the importance of fostering sustainable relationships. By embracing ethical behavior, transparency, and fairness, you will build a reputation as a trustworthy negotiator and forge long-lasting partnerships that extend far beyond the negotiation table.

As you embark on this journey towards negotiation mastery, remember that practice, adaptability, and continuous learning are key. Each chapter of this book will equip you with valuable insights and actionable strategies, bringing you closer to unlocking your full negotiation potential.

Get ready to explore the art, science, and psychology of negotiation. By mastering the principles outlined in this book, you will gain a competitive edge, seize opportunities, and transform the way you approach negotiations, ultimately achieving remarkable results in both your personal and professional endeavors. Let the journey begin!

Chapter 1

The Foundations of Negotiation Mastery

In this chapter, we lay the groundwork for achieving negotiation mastery. We explore the fundamental principles and mindset required to become an effective negotiator.

The Power of Preparation

Thorough preparation is crucial before entering any negotiation as it sets the foundation for success. By investing time and effort in researching the other party, defining your objectives, and determining your negotiation strategy, you can position yourself to make informed decisions and maximize your outcomes. Let's explore the key elements of preparation and illustrate their importance.

Researching the Other Party:

One of the first steps in preparation is gathering information about the other party involved in the negotiation. This includes understanding their background, interests, goals, strengths, weaknesses, and any previous negotiation history. By conducting thorough research, you can uncover valuable insights that may give you an advantage during the negotiation process.

In the business world, mergers and acquisitions (M&A) negotiations require extensive research on the target company. When a multinational corporation considers acquiring a smaller company, they analyze financial records, market position, customer base, and potential synergies. This research helps them understand the target's value, identify potential risks, and negotiate favorable terms. Without proper research, they may overlook critical aspects and make poor decisions during the negotiation.

Defining Objectives:

Before entering a negotiation, it is essential to establish clear and specific objectives. By defining what you want to achieve, you can focus your efforts and communicate your goals effectively. Objectives may include desired outcomes, target prices, specific terms, or any other relevant factors that align with your interests.

In salary negotiations, individuals often define their objectives based on market research, personal needs, and the value they bring to the company. Let's say an employee, Alice, is seeking a promotion and wants to negotiate a higher salary. Through careful research, Alice identifies the average salary range for her desired position in her industry and location. She also considers her experience, skills, and accomplishments. Armed with this information, Alice defines her objective: to secure a salary within the top 10% of the industry average. This specific goal helps Alice during the negotiation, as she can present compelling arguments based on market data and her own value proposition.

Determining Negotiation Strategy:

A well-defined negotiation strategy provides a roadmap for navigating the negotiation process. It involves analyzing potential scenarios, determining your bargaining power, and outlining the tactics and approaches you will employ to achieve your objectives. A thoughtful strategy helps you stay focused, anticipate challenges, and adapt to changing circumstances during the negotiation.

Let's consider a real estate negotiation. A buyer, John, is interested in purchasing a property, but the seller has set a high asking price. John's strategy involves gathering data on comparable properties, understanding market trends, and identifying the seller's motivations. John decides to adopt a collaborative negotiation approach, highlighting the benefits of a quick and smooth transaction for both parties. During the negotiation, he presents the seller with compelling evidence from his research, demonstrating that the asking price is above market value. By employing a well-thought-out negotiation strategy, John is able to secure the property at a fair price.

Understanding Human Psychology

Understanding the psychological aspects of negotiation is essential for effective decision-making and enhancing negotiation skills. Various factors such as cognitive biases, emotional intelligence, and communication techniques play a significant role in shaping the negotiation process. Let's delve into these topics and explore historical scenarios to illustrate their impact.

Cognitive Biases:

Cognitive biases are systematic patterns of deviation from rationality that affect our judgment and decision-making. These biases can influence negotiations by shaping how we perceive information, evaluate options, and make decisions.

The Cuban Missile Crisis of 1962 provides an example of how cognitive biases can impact negotiation outcomes. During the crisis, the United States and the Soviet Union were engaged in a high-stakes negotiation to resolve the presence of Soviet missiles in Cuba. Both parties were susceptible to biases such as the confirmation bias (seeking information that supports existing beliefs) and the overconfidence bias (overestimating the accuracy of their judgments). These biases hindered effective communication and prolonged the negotiation process. It was only when President Kennedy and his advisors recognized and managed these biases that a resolution was reached.

Emotional Intelligence:

Emotional intelligence refers to the ability to recognize, understand, and manage emotions, both in oneself and others. Emotional intelligence plays a vital role in negotiation by enabling individuals to navigate emotions effectively, build rapport, and foster productive relationships.

Nelson Mandela's negotiation skills during the transition of power in South Africa provide an exemplary demonstration of emotional intelligence. Mandela, as a leader of the anti-apartheid movement, possessed the ability to empathize and understand the emotions of both the oppressed and the oppressors. By demonstrating emotional intelligence, he could build trust and forge a productive negotiation process, leading to the dismantling of apartheid and the establishment of a democratic South Africa.

Effective Communication Techniques:

Effective communication is crucial in negotiations as it facilitates understanding, manages conflicts, and persuades others to consider your perspective. Techniques such as active listening, empathy, and assertiveness can enhance communication and positively influence negotiation outcomes.

The Camp David Accords in 1978, mediated by President Jimmy Carter, offer a noteworthy example of effective communication techniques. The negotiations aimed to resolve the Israeli-

Egyptian conflict. Carter employed active listening, empathy, and assertiveness to create an environment conducive to productive dialogue. By understanding the underlying interests and concerns of both parties, Carter facilitated a mutually acceptable agreement, leading to the Egypt-Israel Peace Treaty.

Building Rapport and Trust

Building rapport and trust is an art in negotiation, and it involves strategies that create a positive and cooperative environment, fostering open communication and mutual understanding. Let's explore these strategies and highlight historical scenarios that demonstrate their effectiveness.

Establish a Positive and Cooperative Tone:

Begin the negotiation with a friendly and respectful attitude. One way to establish a positive tone is through the use of humor. Sharing a light-hearted moment or making a relevant joke can help break the ice and create a more relaxed atmosphere.

During the Cold War, the relationship between the United States and the Soviet Union was often tense. However, during the Geneva Summit in 1985, President Ronald Reagan and General Secretary Mikhail Gorbachev used humor to ease tension. Reagan joked about the age difference between them, saying, "I turned 74 today. And as someone reminded me, that's 20 years younger than you, Mr. General Secretary." This lighthearted moment helped establish rapport between the two leaders and set a positive tone for the negotiations.

Active Listening and Empathy:

Active listening is crucial for building rapport and trust. Show genuine interest in the other party's perspective, ask clarifying questions, and provide feedback to demonstrate that you are fully engaged in the conversation. Additionally, practice empathy by trying to understand the emotions and concerns underlying their position.

The Good Friday Agreement negotiations in Northern Ireland, which culminated in 1998, required active listening and empathy. The negotiators had to navigate deep-rooted historical, political, and religious divisions. By actively listening to each other's grievances, concerns, and aspirations, the parties were able to build empathy and develop a shared understanding of the underlying issues. This facilitated a more collaborative negotiation process and ultimately led to the historic agreement.

Transparency and Trustworthiness:
Transparency and trustworthiness are vital for building trust in negotiations. Be open about your intentions, share relevant information, and avoid deceptive tactics. Demonstrating honesty and

integrity creates an environment of trust and encourages reciprocal behavior.

The negotiations between South Africa's apartheid government and anti-apartheid leaders, including Nelson Mandela, showcased the power of transparency and trust. As the negotiations progressed, both sides were transparent about their respective positions, concerns, and aspirations. This transparency helped foster trust and credibility between the parties, leading to more productive negotiations and, eventually, the dismantling of apartheid.

Collaborative Problem-Solving:

Approach the negotiation as a problem-solving exercise rather than a win-lose competition. Collaboratively identify common goals and focus on finding solutions that address the interests of both parties. Encourage brainstorming, explore alternatives, and be open to creative compromises.

The Paris Climate Agreement negotiations in 2015 brought together representatives from nearly 200 countries to address the global challenge of climate change. The negotiators adopted a collaborative problem-solving approach, recognizing that cooperation was essential for achieving meaningful outcomes. Through extensive negotiations, compromises were made, and the agreement was reached, demonstrating the power of collaborative efforts in addressing complex global challenges.

Conclusion

This chapter emphasized the critical importance of thorough preparation in negotiation. By researching the other party, defining objectives, and determining a negotiation strategy, you lay the foundation for successful outcomes.

Thorough preparation equips you with valuable knowledge, confidence, and clarity. Researching the other party allows you to tailor your approach and build rapport. Defining objectives provides a roadmap for success, while determining a negotiation strategy ensures a strategic approach.

By embracing thorough preparation, you position yourself as a skilled negotiator capable of achieving favorable outcomes. As you continue reading, remember that preparation is an ongoing practice, and the principles discussed in this chapter will serve as a solid foundation for your negotiation mastery.

In the upcoming chapters, we will delve into advanced negotiation strategies, handling challenges, and ethical considerations. By integrating these insights into your preparation, you will become a formidable negotiator, navigating any scenario with finesse and achieving optimal results.

Chapter 2

Strategies for Success in Negotiation

In this chapter, we delve into a variety of negotiation strategies that will empower you to achieve successful outcomes in any negotiation scenario.

Win-Win Negotiation

Adopting a collaborative approach in negotiations is key to seeking mutually beneficial solutions that satisfy the interests of both parties involved. This approach emphasizes creating value, problem-solving, and exploring multiple options to maximize joint gains. Let's explore these techniques and highlight historical scenarios to illustrate their effectiveness.

Creating Value:

Instead of focusing solely on dividing a fixed pie, a collaborative approach aims to expand the pie by identifying and creating value that benefits all parties involved. By uncovering shared interests and exploring opportunities for mutual gain, negotiators can find innovative solutions that go beyond initial positions.

The negotiations between Israel and Jordan for a peace treaty in 1994 demonstrated the creation of value. Both countries realized that establishing peaceful relations and economic cooperation would benefit their economies and enhance regional stability. As a result, they explored joint projects such as the development of the Red Sea-Dead Sea Water Conveyance, which involved building a canal to address water scarcity and generate economic opportunities for both nations.

Problem-Solving:

A collaborative approach involves identifying and addressing underlying problems or interests rather than focusing on positions. By delving into the root causes of the issues, negotiators can work together to find creative solutions that meet both parties' needs and build sustainable agreements.

The negotiation of the Dayton Agreement in 1995, which ended the Bosnian War, exemplified problem-solving. The conflict involved complex ethnic, political, and territorial issues. The negotiators shifted their focus from entrenched positions to addressing the underlying concerns of each party. Through extensive negotiations, they developed a power-sharing arrangement, territorial compromises, and provisions for human rights protection, laying the foundation for peace and stability in Bosnia and Herzegovina.

Exploring Multiple Options:

A collaborative approach encourages the exploration of multiple options to find win-win solutions. By considering various alternatives and being open to creative compromises, negotiators can expand the range of possible outcomes and increase the likelihood of reaching mutually beneficial agreements.

The negotiations that led to the Oslo Accords in 1993 between Israel and the Palestine Liberation Organization (PLO) exemplify exploring multiple options. The negotiators engaged in intensive discussions and considered various proposals to address the complex issues of Israeli-Palestinian relations. Through flexibility, creativity, and a willingness to explore different options, they reached a historic agreement that included provisions for Palestinian self-governance and paved the way for further negotiations on a final settlement.

Competitive Negotiation Tactics

Handling competitive negotiators and contentious situations requires strategies to assert your interests, set boundaries, and employ persuasive techniques while maintaining a constructive negotiation process and preserving the relationship. Let's explore these strategies and highlight historical scenarios to emphasize their effectiveness.

Prepare Thoroughly:

Thorough preparation is crucial when dealing with competitive negotiators. Gather as much information as possible about the other party's interests, positions, and potential tactics. Anticipate their arguments and objections, and develop strong counterarguments supported by relevant facts and data. Being well-prepared enhances your confidence and ability to navigate contentious situations effectively.

The negotiation between the United States and the Soviet Union during the Cold War provides an example of dealing with competitive negotiators. Both parties were engaged in high-stakes negotiations, often with competing interests and contentious issues. Thorough preparation, including understanding each other's nuclear capabilities and strategic goals, helped negotiators navigate the complexities and find common ground, leading to important arms control agreements like the Strategic Arms Limitation Talks (SALT) and the Intermediate-Range Nuclear Forces Treaty (INF Treaty).

Maintain Calm and Composure:

In contentious situations, it is essential to stay calm and composed. Avoid reacting impulsively or becoming overly defensive. Instead, maintain a professional demeanor and focus on the issues at hand. By staying composed, you demonstrate your ability to handle difficult situations and maintain control of the negotiation process.

The negotiations between North Korea and the international community regarding its nuclear program exemplify the importance of maintaining composure. These negotiations were often tense and emotionally charged. Diplomats from various countries had to navigate through heated exchanges and provocative rhetoric. By maintaining composure and diplomatic professionalism, negotiators were able to continue engaging in dialogue and seeking potential solutions.

Assert Your Interests and Set Boundaries:
When dealing with competitive negotiators, it is crucial to assert your interests and set clear boundaries. Clearly communicate your objectives, needs, and limitations. Avoid being overly accommodating or conceding too much without receiving value in return. By asserting your interests and setting boundaries, you establish a framework for the negotiation that ensures your needs are taken into account.

The negotiations during the World Trade Organization (WTO) Doha Round provide an example of asserting interests and setting boundaries. The negotiations involved multiple countries with diverse economic interests. Developing countries asserted their interests by emphasizing the importance of fair trade, reducing agricultural subsidies, and addressing trade imbalances. Through assertiveness and setting boundaries, they aimed to ensure their concerns were addressed within the negotiation process.

Employ Persuasive Techniques:

Effective persuasive techniques can help navigate contentious situations without damaging the relationship. Use logical arguments, evidence, and examples to support your position. Appeal to shared interests and values to find common ground. Employ active listening and empathy to understand the other party's perspective and adapt your persuasive approach accordingly.

The negotiations leading to the Iran Nuclear Deal in 2015 involved contentious issues and strong opposing views. Persuasive techniques were employed to bridge the gaps and reach a consensus. Diplomats utilized various persuasive approaches, including emphasizing shared security concerns, presenting verifiable inspections mechanisms, and highlighting the potential economic benefits of the agreement. These techniques helped build understanding and persuade stakeholders to support the deal.

Negotiating in Complex Situations

Negotiating in complex scenarios, such as multi-party negotiations, mergers and acquisitions, and international business deals, requires specific skills to manage diverse interests, cultural differences, and complex power dynamics. Let's explore these skills and highlight historical scenarios to emphasize their importance.

Managing Diverse Interests:

In complex negotiations involving multiple parties, it is crucial to manage diverse interests effectively. Seek to understand the priorities and motivations of each party involved and look for areas of overlap and potential trade-offs. Facilitate open and transparent communication to ensure all perspectives are heard and integrated into the negotiation process.

The negotiation of the Paris Climate Agreement in 2015 involved representatives from nearly 200 countries with diverse interests. Negotiators had to manage the interests of developed and developing countries, balancing the need for climate action with economic considerations. By creating a platform for dialogue and collaboration, negotiators were able to find common ground and reach a historic agreement.

Navigating Cultural Differences:

In international negotiations, cultural differences can play a significant role. Understanding and respecting cultural norms, communication styles, and decision-making processes is essential. Adapt your approach to accommodate cultural diversity, and invest time in building relationships and trust with individuals from different cultural backgrounds.

The negotiation between the United States and China for China's entry into the World Trade Organization (WTO) in the early 2000s provides an example of navigating cultural differences. The negotiation involved significant differences in economic systems, political ideologies, and cultural values. Skilled negotiators recognized and respected these differences, working to bridge gaps and find mutually beneficial solutions that led to China's accession to the WTO.

Managing Complex Power Dynamics:
In negotiations involving mergers and acquisitions or other complex business deals, power dynamics can be intricate.

Identify key stakeholders, understand their interests and influence, and develop strategies to manage power dynamics effectively. Seek win-win solutions that satisfy the interests of both powerful and less powerful parties involved.

The negotiation between Disney and 21st Century Fox for the acquisition of Fox's entertainment assets in 2017-2019 exemplifies managing complex power dynamics. The negotiation involved two major media conglomerates with significant market presence and diverse assets. Skilled negotiators from both sides navigated power imbalances, addressing concerns related to regulatory approvals, competition, and shareholder interests. The negotiation resulted in a successful acquisition that reshaped the media landscape.

Building Trust and Long-Term Relationships:
In complex negotiations, building trust and cultivating long-term relationships is essential. Invest time and effort in developing personal connections, demonstrating integrity, and delivering on commitments. Foster a collaborative and mutually beneficial approach that establishes a foundation for future interactions.

The negotiation between Microsoft and LinkedIn for Microsoft's acquisition of the professional networking platform in 2016 showcases the importance of building trust and long-term relationships. The negotiation involved Microsoft's desire to expand its digital ecosystem and LinkedIn's interest in accessing new resources and markets. By building trust through open and transparent communication and demonstrating a shared vision for the future, negotiators were able to reach a deal that benefited both companies.

Conclusion

This chapter emphasized the significance of effective communication in negotiation. We explored skills such as active listening, strategic questioning, and clear and persuasive communication. By mastering these skills, you can enhance your negotiation outcomes and build stronger relationships.

Effective communication is the cornerstone of successful negotiation. It fosters understanding, trust, and collaboration. Active listening enables empathy and establishes a foundation of mutual respect. Strategic questioning uncovers underlying interests and promotes creative problem-solving.

Clear and persuasive communication allows you to articulate your positions effectively and influence the other party. It involves delivering messages with clarity, supporting them with compelling arguments, and being aware of nonverbal cues. Developing strong communication skills enhances your ability to navigate negotiations successfully.

Continuing on your path to negotiation mastery, remember that communication is an ongoing practice. Practice active listening, refine your questioning techniques, and work on delivering clear and persuasive messages. Advanced communication strategies and ethical considerations will be explored in the upcoming chapters.

By mastering effective communication, you position yourself as a confident and influential negotiator, capable of achieving successful outcomes. It is through effective communication that you build rapport, understand the other party's perspective, and navigate complex negotiation scenarios.

In summary, effective communication is vital for negotiation mastery. By honing your communication skills strategically, you become a more influential negotiator, achieving optimal results in various negotiation contexts.

Chapter 3
Overcoming Challenges and Difficult Negotiators

Negotiation often presents challenges, including difficult counterparts and unexpected obstacles. This chapter equips you with the skills necessary to overcome such challenges and achieve favorable outcomes.

Dealing with Difficult Personalities

Navigating negotiations with difficult personalities, including aggressive negotiators, manipulative individuals, and those resistant to compromise, requires specific strategies to defuse tension and maintain control of the negotiation process. Let's explore these strategies and highlight historical scenarios to emphasize their effectiveness.

Stay Calm and Composed:

When dealing with difficult personalities, it is crucial to remain calm and composed. Avoid getting caught up in their aggressive or manipulative tactics. By maintaining your composure, you can think clearly, respond strategically, and maintain control of the negotiation process.

The negotiations during the Cuban Missile Crisis in 1962 provide an example of staying calm in the face of aggression. The United States and the Soviet Union were engaged in high-stakes negotiations that could have escalated into a full-scale nuclear war. Despite the intense pressure and aggressive posturing, both sides managed to stay composed, leading to a diplomatic resolution that diffused the crisis.

Focus on Interests, Not Personalities:

When negotiating with difficult personalities, it is important to focus on the underlying interests rather than getting caught up in personal dynamics. Identify their motivations and concerns and try to find common ground based on shared interests. By shifting the focus away from personalities, you can redirect the negotiation towards constructive problem-solving.

The negotiations to end the apartheid regime in South Africa provide an example of focusing on interests rather than personal dynamics. The negotiations involved various parties with deeply entrenched positions and personal animosities. However, by shifting the focus to the common interest of achieving a peaceful and inclusive society, negotiators were able to overcome personal differences and reach a historic agreement.

Set Clear Boundaries:

In negotiations with difficult personalities, it is important to set clear boundaries and assert your position. Clearly communicate your objectives and red lines, and do not allow yourself to be manipulated or coerced into unfavorable agreements. By setting boundaries, you establish a framework for negotiation and maintain control over the process.

The negotiations between Greece and its international creditors during the Greek debt crisis provide an example of setting clear boundaries. The negotiations were characterized by tense discussions and conflicting demands. Greek negotiators set clear boundaries by asserting their country's need for economic stability and social welfare. By maintaining their position, they were able to negotiate a compromise that addressed their concerns.

Seek Mediation or Third-Party Assistance:

In some cases, involving a mediator or seeking third-party assistance can be effective when dealing with difficult personalities. A neutral third party can help defuse tensions, facilitate communication, and guide the negotiation towards a resolution. Their presence can provide a sense of objectivity and fairness, promoting a more constructive negotiation process.

The negotiations between Israel and Palestine mediated by the United States provide an example of involving a third party. The negotiations were often characterized by deep-rooted mistrust and contentious issues. The presence of a neutral mediator helped create a more conducive environment for dialogue and problem-solving, increasing the chances of reaching a mutually acceptable agreement.

Managing Emotional Situations

The impact of emotions in negotiation is significant, as they can influence decision-making, communication, and the overall outcome of the negotiation. Developing techniques to manage both your own emotions and those of the other party is essential for maintaining composure, diffusing tension, and fostering productive dialogue, even in high-stress situations. Let's explore these techniques and highlight real-life historical scenarios to emphasize their importance.

Self-Regulation and Emotional Awareness:

Self-regulation involves recognizing and managing your own emotions during a negotiation. It is crucial to be aware of your emotional state and its potential impact on your decision-making and communication. Practice techniques such as deep breathing, taking breaks when needed, and reframing negative emotions to maintain composure and think clearly.

The negotiation to end the Iran Hostage Crisis in 1980 provides an example of self-regulation and emotional awareness. During the negotiations, tensions ran high, and emotions were intense due to the prolonged hostage situation. Skilled negotiators on both sides demonstrated emotional awareness by managing their own emotions, focusing on the negotiation objectives, and working towards a peaceful resolution.

Active Listening and Empathy:

Active listening and empathy are vital in managing emotions and fostering productive dialogue. Pay attention to the other party's concerns, perspectives, and underlying emotions. Validate their feelings and demonstrate empathy by acknowledging their viewpoints. This helps create a sense of understanding and builds trust, leading to more constructive negotiations.

The negotiation between Nelson Mandela and the South African government for the peaceful transition from apartheid to democracy exemplifies the importance of active listening and empathy. Mandela actively listened to the concerns of the government officials and acknowledged their fears and interests. By demonstrating empathy, he helped create an atmosphere of trust and understanding, ultimately leading to a successful negotiation and the dismantling of apartheid.

Emotionally Intelligent Communication:
Emotionally intelligent communication involves effectively expressing emotions and managing the emotions of others. Use clear and assertive communication techniques while being mindful of the impact your words may have on the emotional state of the other party.

Choose words carefully, maintain a respectful tone, and focus on problem-solving rather than personal attacks.

The negotiation between Israel and Egypt for the Camp David Accords in 1978 demonstrates the importance of emotionally intelligent communication. The negotiations were complex and emotionally charged due to years of conflict and mistrust. Skilled negotiators utilized emotionally intelligent communication to convey their interests and concerns while remaining respectful and constructive. This facilitated open dialogue and ultimately led to the signing of a historic peace agreement.

Collaboration and Building Win-Win Solutions:
Fostering a collaborative mindset and seeking win-win solutions can help manage emotions effectively. By focusing on shared interests and exploring mutually beneficial outcomes, you can

create an environment where emotions are channeled towards finding creative solutions rather than escalating conflicts.

The negotiation between Microsoft and the Department of Justice during the antitrust case in the late 1990s illustrates the importance of collaboration and win-win solutions. Emotions were high as the negotiations addressed critical issues related to competition and market dominance. By adopting a collaborative approach and finding common ground, the negotiation resulted in a settlement that addressed concerns from both sides and allowed Microsoft to continue operating with certain restrictions.

Conclusion:

This chapter emphasized the importance of a collaborative mindset and a win-win approach in negotiations. Collaboration fosters creative problem-solving and builds strong relationships, leading to mutually beneficial outcomes.

By shifting from a competitive mindset to a collaborative one, you open opportunities for success. Principles such as focusing on interests, separating people from the problem, generating options, and using objective criteria guide effective negotiation.

Building strong relationships with the other party is key. Investing in rapport, empathy, and finding common ground creates a positive and collaborative atmosphere. These relationships facilitate communication, trust, and cooperation for achieving optimal results.

As you strive for negotiation mastery, remember the value of a collaborative mindset. Prioritize open communication, shared interests, and creative solutions. By fostering win-win outcomes, you establish yourself as a trusted negotiator capable of achieving success.

Chapter 4
Advanced Negotiation Techniques

In this chapter, we explore advanced techniques that will take your negotiation skills to the next level, allowing you to tackle complex challenges and achieve exceptional results.

The Power of Persuasion

The art of persuasion and influence is a powerful tool in negotiation, allowing individuals to sway opinions and shape outcomes in their favor. By effectively leveraging persuasive techniques such as framing, storytelling, and building coalitions, negotiators can enhance their ability to influence others. Let's explore these techniques and highlight historical scenarios to emphasize their impact.

Framing:

Framing involves presenting information in a way that influences how it is perceived and interpreted. By framing the negotiation issues, arguments, and proposals in a favorable light, negotiators can shape the perspectives and attitudes of the other party.

The negotiation of the Good Friday Agreement in 1998, which aimed to resolve the conflict in Northern Ireland, demonstrates the power of framing. Negotiators framed the agreement as a pathway to peace, emphasizing the benefits of a shared future and inclusivity. By framing the negotiation in a positive light, they influenced public opinion and garnered support for the agreement, ultimately leading to its successful implementation.

Storytelling:

Storytelling is a persuasive technique that engages emotions and helps convey complex ideas in a relatable and memorable way. By crafting compelling narratives that illustrate the impact and benefits of certain outcomes, negotiators can capture the attention and empathy of the other party.

The negotiation of the Paris Climate Agreement in 2015 utilized storytelling to persuade and inspire. Through powerful narratives, negotiators shared stories of communities affected by climate change, highlighting the urgency and moral imperative for action. By connecting emotionally with the other parties, they successfully garnered support and commitment to address climate change on a global scale.

Building Coalitions:

Building coalitions involves forming alliances or partnerships with other individuals or groups who share similar interests or goals. By uniting with like-minded parties, negotiators can amplify their influence and present a unified front, increasing their persuasive power.

Real-life scenario: The negotiation of the Joint Comprehensive Plan of Action (JCPOA), also known as the Iran Nuclear Deal, in 2015 exemplifies the use of coalition building. Negotiators from multiple countries, including the United States, Iran, and several European powers, formed a coalition to address Iran's nuclear program. By presenting a united front and leveraging collective influence, they successfully reached an agreement that restricted Iran's nuclear activities.

Building Credibility and Trust:
Credibility and trust are essential for effective persuasion and influence. Establishing a reputation for integrity, expertise, and reliability enhances the persuasiveness of negotiators. By consistently demonstrating credibility and building trust through transparent

communication, delivering on promises, and maintaining ethical conduct, negotiators can gain the confidence of the other party.

The negotiation between the United States and the Soviet Union during the Cold War demonstrates the importance of credibility and trust. Through various negotiations, such as the Strategic Arms Limitation Talks (SALT), negotiators on both sides worked to build trust and establish credibility. By demonstrating a commitment to arms control and consistently honoring agreements, they were able to reduce tensions and achieve significant progress in nuclear disarmament.

Negotiating with High-Stakes

Negotiating in high-stakes situations requires specific strategies to navigate the pressure and limited margin for error. Let's explore techniques such as risk assessment, strategic concessions, and leveraging alternatives, and highlight historical scenarios to emphasize their effectiveness in securing optimal outcomes.

Risk Assessment:

In high-stakes negotiations, conducting a thorough risk assessment is crucial. Identify the potential risks and uncertainties associated with the negotiation, including legal, financial, and reputational risks. By understanding the potential consequences and developing contingency plans, you can make informed decisions and mitigate risks effectively.

The negotiation between the United States and the Soviet Union during the Cuban Missile Crisis in 1962 serves as a notable example of risk assessment. The stakes were incredibly high, with the risk of nuclear war. Through a careful assessment of the risks involved, both parties realized the catastrophic consequences and chose a diplomatic resolution to prevent further escalation.

Strategic Concessions:

Strategic concessions involve making calculated compromises to achieve overall favorable outcomes. Identify the key priorities and areas where you can make concessions without compromising your core interests. By strategically offering concessions, you can build goodwill, maintain momentum in the negotiation, and create an environment conducive to reaching mutually beneficial agreements.

The negotiation leading to the Oslo Accords in 1993 between Israel and Palestine demonstrates the use of strategic concessions. Both parties made significant compromises to overcome deep-rooted conflicts and move towards a peaceful resolution. By strategically offering concessions, such as mutual recognition and limited self-governance, they established trust and laid the foundation for further negotiations.

Leveraging Alternatives:

Having alternatives or BATNA (Best Alternative to a Negotiated Agreement) is crucial in high-stakes negotiations. Assess and strengthen your BATNA by developing viable alternatives outside of the current negotiation. By leveraging alternatives, you gain leverage, maintain a sense of control, and avoid being overly dependent on a single outcome.

The negotiation between Microsoft and the European Union in the early 2000s regarding antitrust concerns exemplifies the use of leveraging alternatives. Microsoft's alternative was to continue operating without making substantial concessions. This allowed them to negotiate from a position of strength and secure more favorable terms in the final agreement.

Building Relationships and Coalitions:

In high-stakes negotiations, building relationships and coalitions can be instrumental. Identify potential allies or stakeholders who share common interests or objectives. By forming strategic alliances, you can amplify your influence, increase your leverage, and present a unified front, enhancing the chances of achieving optimal outcomes.

The negotiation leading to the Paris Climate Agreement in 2015 involved multiple countries coming together to address climate change. By building relationships and forming coalitions, negotiators created a collective voice and increased the impact of their demands. This led to a comprehensive agreement with commitments from a large number of nations.

Conclusion

This chapter explored the art of conflict resolution and managing difficult negotiators. By adopting constructive approaches, managing emotions, and employing effective strategies, you can navigate conflicts and challenging personalities with confidence.

Conflict is an inherent part of negotiations, and handling it skillfully is crucial. By embracing a principled and collaborative approach, conflicts can become opportunities for finding mutually beneficial solutions.

Managing emotions is essential in conflict resolution. By understanding and controlling emotions, as well as empathizing with the other party, you create a productive negotiation environment and foster better communication.

Dealing with difficult negotiators requires adaptability and strategic approaches. Understanding their motivations, managing their tactics, and maintaining focus on your objectives are key to steering the negotiation towards a positive outcome.

As you continue your journey to negotiation mastery, remember the importance of honing conflict resolution skills and strategies for managing difficult negotiators. These skills will empower you to navigate complex negotiation scenarios with resilience.

In summary, this chapter highlighted the significance of effective conflict resolution and managing difficult negotiators. By adopting constructive approaches, managing emotions, and employing strategic strategies, you position yourself as a confident negotiator capable of achieving successful outcomes in any negotiation context.

Chapter 5
Negotiation Ethics and Creating Sustainable Relationships

In the final chapter, we explore the ethical dimension of negotiation and the importance of building long-term, sustainable relationships with your negotiation counterparts.

Ethical Considerations

Ethical dilemmas can arise in negotiation when there is a conflict between achieving desired outcomes and maintaining ethical standards. Navigating these dilemmas with integrity is essential for fostering fairness, transparency, and trustworthiness throughout the negotiation process. Let's explore these concepts and highlight real-life historical scenarios to emphasize the importance of ethical behavior.

Fairness:

Fairness involves treating all parties involved in the negotiation equitably and without bias. It requires considering the interests and perspectives of all stakeholders and avoiding unfair advantage or exploitation.

The negotiation for the release of hostages during the Iran-Contra affair in the 1980s presents an ethical dilemma related to fairness. The United States faced the challenge of negotiating with Iran while simultaneously providing military support to the Contras in Nicaragua. This raised concerns about fairness, as negotiations with Iran might have been influenced by unrelated political considerations. Resolving this dilemma required maintaining fairness by separating the two issues and ensuring that negotiations were conducted solely on the basis of resolving the hostage situation.

Transparency:

Transparency involves openness and honesty in sharing information, intentions, and motives during the negotiation process. It requires clear and accurate communication to build trust and foster an environment of mutual understanding.

The negotiation of the Good Friday Agreement in Northern Ireland in 1998 encountered ethical dilemmas related to transparency. The negotiators faced challenges in dealing with sensitive issues and addressing historical grievances. However, by maintaining transparency and openly discussing the concerns of all parties, they fostered trust and increased the likelihood of reaching a sustainable agreement.

Trustworthiness:

Trustworthiness is essential in negotiation and involves demonstrating reliability, keeping promises, and acting in good faith. It requires honoring agreements, maintaining confidentiality when necessary, and avoiding deceptive tactics.

The negotiation between the United States and the Soviet Union during the Strategic Arms Limitation Talks (SALT) in the 1970s exemplifies the importance of trustworthiness. Both parties needed to rely on accurate information and assurances regarding arms control measures. By demonstrating trustworthiness, such as verifying compliance and upholding agreements, negotiators built mutual trust and contributed to the stability of the negotiations.

Ethical Decision-Making:

Ethical decision-making involves considering the moral implications of various choices and selecting actions that align with ethical principles. It requires balancing competing interests, avoiding harm, and upholding ethical standards even in challenging situations.

The negotiation surrounding the adoption of the Universal Declaration of Human Rights by the United Nations in 1948 encountered ethical dilemmas related to balancing cultural relativism and universal human rights. Negotiators faced challenges in reconciling diverse cultural perspectives with the need for universally recognized human rights. Resolving this dilemma required ethical decision-making, acknowledging the importance of cultural diversity while upholding fundamental human rights principles.

Creating Win-Win Partnerships

Forging win-win partnerships in negotiation is essential for creating long-lasting relationships and ensuring mutual success. By adopting strategies that prioritize collaboration, trust, and mutual benefits, negotiators can establish strong partnerships that extend beyond individual negotiations. Let's explore these strategies and highlight historical scenarios to emphasize the value of win-win partnerships.

Building Trust and Rapport:

Building trust is fundamental in forging win-win partnerships. It involves establishing credibility, maintaining open communication, and demonstrating reliability. By investing time and effort in building rapport, negotiators can foster a foundation of trust that strengthens the partnership.

The negotiation between Nelson Mandela and F. W. de Klerk during the transition from apartheid to democracy in South Africa exemplifies the importance of trust and rapport. Mandela and de Klerk worked together to negotiate a peaceful end to apartheid and establish a democratic government. Their ability to build trust and develop a strong working relationship played a crucial role in the successful transition and their subsequent collaboration in building a new South Africa.

Seeking Mutual Benefit:

Win-win partnerships are based on the principle of mutual benefit, where both parties strive to achieve outcomes that satisfy their respective interests. By identifying common goals and shared benefits, negotiators can create solutions that go beyond immediate gains and foster collaboration for long-term success.

The negotiation between Microsoft and Intel in the 1990s provides an example of seeking mutual benefit. Both companies recognized the potential synergy between their technologies and collaborated to optimize software and hardware performance. By working together, they achieved mutual success, driving innovation and dominating the personal computer industry.

Long-Term Relationship Building:

Win-win partnerships extend beyond individual negotiations and focus on building long-term relationships. By nurturing ongoing communication, addressing concerns proactively, and consistently delivering on commitments, negotiators can strengthen the partnership and lay the foundation for future collaboration.

The strategic partnership between Apple and Samsung in the early 2010s highlights the value of long-term relationship building. Despite being competitors in certain areas, Apple relied on Samsung for the supply of key components. By fostering a strong relationship and ensuring reliable supply, both companies benefited from the collaboration and sustained their partnership for several years.

Collaborative Problem-Solving:

Win-win partnerships emphasize collaborative problem-solving, where both parties actively engage in finding creative and mutually beneficial solutions. By cncouraging open dialogue, brainstorming options, and considering multiple perspectives, negotiators can overcome challenges and maximize joint gains.

The negotiation leading to the Camp David Accords in 1978 between Israel and Egypt demonstrates the power of collaborative problem-solving. Negotiators engaged in intense discussions, exploring various options and compromises to resolve long-standing conflicts. By adopting a collaborative approach, they reached an agreement that established peace between the two nations and reshaped the dynamics of the Middle East.

Conclusion

This chapter highlighted the importance of ethical considerations in negotiation. By embracing fairness, integrity, and trustworthiness, we create an environment of collaboration and build strong relationships. Ethical behavior not only aligns with our moral compass but also contributes to long-term success and a positive reputation.

Maintaining ethical standards is crucial throughout the negotiation process. Strategies for navigating ethical dilemmas, such as addressing conflicts of interest and ensuring transparent communication, were explored. By actively incorporating ethical considerations, we elevate the integrity of our negotiations.

As you strive for negotiation mastery, prioritize ethical behavior. Embrace fairness, integrity, and trust as guiding principles. By doing so, you establish yourself as a respected negotiator, capable of achieving successful outcomes while upholding the highest ethical standards.

In summary, this chapter underscored the significance of ethical considerations in negotiation. By embodying fairness, integrity, and trustworthiness, we foster collaboration, build relationships, and achieve sustainable agreements. Prioritizing ethical behavior is essential for long-term success and maintaining a positive reputation as skilled negotiators.

Chapter 6
The Path to Negotiation Mastery

Congratulations! You have embarked on a transformative journey towards negotiation mastery. Throughout this book, we have explored the essential principles, strategies, and skills that lay the foundation for becoming a skilled negotiator. In this final chapter, we will reflect on your progress and outline the path to continued growth and success in negotiation.

Reflecting on Your Journey

Take a moment to reflect on how far you've come. You have learned the importance of thorough preparation, effective communication, collaborative approaches, conflict resolution, and ethical considerations in negotiations. Each chapter has equipped you with valuable insights and practical techniques that can be applied to a variety of negotiation scenarios.

Embracing Continuous Improvement

Negotiation mastery is a journey that knows no end. To continue honing your skills and achieving even greater heights, it is essential to embrace a mindset of continuous improvement. Cultivate a curiosity for learning, seek feedback from others, and stay up to date with the latest trends and research in negotiation.

Sharpening Your Skills

Refine and expand your negotiation toolkit by exploring advanced techniques and strategies. Delve into specialized areas such as cross-cultural negotiations, multi-party negotiations, and negotiations in high-stakes situations. By broadening your understanding and adaptability, you will be prepared to navigate diverse and complex negotiation challenges.

Learning from Experience

One of the most valuable sources of growth is learning from real-life experiences. Actively seek opportunities to apply your negotiation skills in various settings. Reflect on each negotiation, analyze the outcomes, and identify areas for improvement. Embrace both successes and failures as valuable learning opportunities that will contribute to your growth as a negotiator.

Building a Network

Networking plays a crucial role in negotiation mastery. Connect with fellow negotiators, join professional associations, and participate in negotiation-focused events. Engage in discussions, share experiences, and learn from others' perspectives. Building a network of like-minded individuals will not only provide support but also foster opportunities for collaboration and knowledge sharing.

Becoming an Ethical Leader

As you continue your journey, remember the importance of ethical behavior. Use your negotiation skills to promote fairness, integrity, and trust in all your interactions. Lead by example and inspire others to embrace ethical conduct in negotiations. By doing so, you will not only achieve success but also contribute to a positive and sustainable negotiation environment.

Conclusion

Negotiation mastery is a lifelong pursuit, marked by continuous learning, growth, and self-improvement. By integrating the principles, strategies, and skills discussed in this book, you are well on your way to becoming a skilled negotiator capable of achieving successful outcomes in a wide range of negotiation scenarios.

Remember to approach negotiations with thorough preparation, effective communication, a collaborative mindset, conflict resolution skills, and a commitment to ethical conduct. Embrace the challenges and embrace each negotiation as an opportunity for growth.

As you conclude this book, keep the lessons learned close to heart and embark on your ongoing journey towards negotiation mastery. With dedication, practice, and a passion for continuous improvement, you will unlock the full potential of your negotiation skills and achieve remarkable results in both your personal and professional life.

Thank you for joining us on this transformative journey. May your negotiation mastery empower you to navigate the complexities of the negotiation landscape with confidence, integrity, and exceptional outcomes.

www.ingramcontent.com/pod-product-compliance
Lightning Source LLC
Chambersburg PA
CBHW072032230526
45466CB00020B/1753